you will not control me

A collection by:

Linda M. Crate

acknowledgements

anchors of pain and rage was first published in the anthology War Crimes Against the Uterus.

legendary, mythical phoenix was first published in Voice of Eve.

the sirens lament was first published in Cauldron Anthology.

who is the serpent? was first published in Less Than A Man.

will never be their songbird was first published in Junto Magazine.

Contents

femininity isn't fragile 7

anchors of pain and rage 8

legendary, mythical phoenix 9

society isn't right 10

my fires can burn 11

a woman isn't your property 12

the siren's lament 13

spinning webs 15

bible lesson for misogynists 16

it's not up to you 17

let us love them 18

they don't care about living people 19

a woman owes no one 20

who is the serpent? 21

those without substance 23

you no longer care 24

we deserve more 25

this isn't black and white 26

hypothetical lives 27

in case you were wondering 28

you are the modern day pharisees 29

your life matters to me 30

they are already here 31

it's a pity then that you're wrong 32

women are always the villains 33

you don't value life 34

you do not value women 35

i refuse to be caged 36

will never be their songbird 37

we will not be destroyed 39

we were all given free will 41

i refuse to be oppressed 42
they already have heartbeats 43
i will fight for justice 44
open up your eyes 45
so leave her alone 46
you aren't better than anyone else 47
you can't force the "right" choice 48
i will never accept that 49
a woman shouldn't have to abandon herself 51
treat others as you would treat yourself 52
stop throwing your stones 53
they're not devils 54
a time for war 55
you're blinded by your feelings 56
you're practicing wrong 57
these women have faces 58
don't really believe in life, do you? 59
i cannot forgive nightmares or hell 60
we were never inferiors 61
battle ready wild birds 62
whether you like it or not 63
we can all be monsters 64
sometimes life gives us no choice 65
you feel the need to oppress others 67
we won't let this go 68
it isn't about babies 69
more than our circumstances 70
you choose to be blind 71
i have so much rage, as is 72
i have little faith in them 74
they are devils not gods 75
our lives are our own 76

femininity isn't fragile

there is nothing fragile
about
femininity,
we are the ones that
give birth;
we are the ones that endure
periods and menopause
and a thousand other things
that men will never know—
i don't hate men,
but i do not like men like you
so offended over the
most simple of things;
if you consider women to be
such a weakness
perhaps tell your mother
she has no strength
i bet you won't—
sew shut your lips
i am done hearing about how awful women are,
we are all trying our best to get through this thing
called life;
we will not be sorry for demanding dignity and respect
that we should have always been given.
-linda m. crate

anchors of pain and rage

these bills aren't about babies,
but control;
and the fact some people
refuse to see that
makes my blood boil even hotter
than the bills themselves—
it's as if they seem to think of women
as nothing more than property,
that it is okay to enslave a person to their
needs;
their bloated sense of ego
or their emotions are allowed to dictate
laws—
i will always be pro-choice
because i believe it is no one's business
what you do with your life but your own
in the end we don't have to answer to other people in
the afterlife,
and so why all this judgment and this hate and this rage against
women?
we are magical, powerful, divine creatures and if it is a war they
truly want then we will sink their ships with all the
anchors of our pain and rage.
- linda m. crate

legendary, mythical phoenix

you can sculpt a thousand
pedestals and gilded cages
for me,
but i will never be held in the restraints
of who people wish me to be;
i am a sunset,
raven,
valkyrie of white wings,
keeper of golden suns,
daughter of the silver moon—
a lie no matter how
ornamented is still a lie
so i won't sit
in the boxes society says are mine
for i am of a worth more infinite
than rubies or diamonds,
and my magic will not be shattered
nor dimmed by the fallacy
of their lies;
my voice will always rise from the ashes
for like the legendary mythical phoenix
i will rise immortal of the flame
burning every nightmare and monster
who ever stood in the way of my dreams.
- linda m. crate

society isn't right

i don't care what society wants, they are not always right, i will not follow the crowd but my own dreams; i am who i am and i will not make an apology for that—women should be allowed to make waves, to have dreams, and to follow their ambitions without being belittled or made to feel guilty; not everyone dreams of being a mother—why should anyone force my hand? you are pro-birth not pro-life, only want control; and that i will resist because my body and my life are my own—no one will dictate what i do, i will not be enslaved by the needs of the patriarchy; they are only looking to make every woman a felon so they cannot vote—they want to silence us, but i am done being silenced; all my youth i held my tongue so now i will rage and roar with all the force of a hurricane, i am the daughter of the moon; i will forever shine light so that even in the darkness someone can have hope because i know not everyone is fierce as i—so i will blow the trumpet and wield the sword for all those that cannot, anyone who seeks to own a woman will be met in a furious rage; i am the daughter of a monster—i will spare them no mercy, they should be terrified because women are stronger than they give us credit for; we will not bend our knees to pray for they are but men and not gods—the world owes you nothing and neither do we.

-linda m. crate

my fires can burn

you won't strike
down my temples
nor steal from me
my divinity
you won't steal away
my magic or my light
i am a phoenix
my tears may heal,
but my fires can burn a man
to ashes from which he will
not rise;
i don't owe you anything
for existing—
i don't owe you anything
just because you find me
attractive
or want to know me better,
and i won't be made to feel guilty
for ignoring advances from
anyone
i have no interest in;
women aren't your immediate tools
of sexual gratification, your wombs
for hire or rent, your broodmares,
or your moral compasses—
we exist in order to create a world
far superior to the one we know as ours.
-linda m. crate

a woman isn't your property

you don't own me, nor will you consume me; i am not your feast of flesh—i am a woman powerful and divine, won't surrender to anyone; my magic and my light are to help those whom seek to follow their dreams—i am more than the sum of my body parts, and i support a woman's right to choose their own path in life; don't lecture me—you are not to cast stones unless you are without sin, so stop with your judgment; you know not what someone is facing and you cannot dictate how someone lives their life—we were all given free will, and i won't let anyone take that away from anyone; won't let anyone be enslaved by the needs of society if i can help it—i will fight tooth and nail so people can make their own choices, life their own lives, and keep their own dignity; no person should be owned by another person—we should all have our freedom, our beating hearts are our own; our songs and our paths are our own; our bodies should be our own as well—just because a woman exists doesn't make her your property or means she owes you anything.

-linda m. crate

the siren's lament

my soul is one of song
prose and poetry
dance in my heart and mind
both,
and you were my favorite
song for a time;
but you always spurned my sexual
advances unless you were
in the mood
too—
once you told me that i was
a succubus,
but i have always been a siren because
music and water touch every point
of my soul;
i wanted you to be my heart's duet
the melody in me that
never died—
i wanted you fully as i gave myself
fully to you,
but i was always told that i was too
driven and too focused upon
my sexual appetites
that i should pray for redemption;
but why should i be
shamed for feeling the same way you did
for me?
i suppose it's because i'm a woman
that i should want to be

something innocent and pure,
but i have always been a shade of grey;
honesty, love, and light with a thousand flaws
yet beautiful in my own way.
- linda m. crate

spinning webs

we live in a world where women
must remain pure and untainted,
but men can be depraved;
and what incentive is that to want
to play into society's needs
of marriage and childbirth?
why should i want a family if i will
be seen as something less than human,
and my husband is expected to rule
over me with an iron fist?
i am not the type of woman that you tame,
and i know i cannot be the only one;
wild birds flying against the wind
sharpened talons
ready to take the eyes of any who would
shatter their dreams—
why is it in a civilized country women
cannot even rule over their own lives,
to be their own monsters, to have rights and say
over their own bodies?
it's disgusting the hypocrisy
a woman is to be beautiful and untouched
but a man can be filthy in heart and mind,
she is to be his moral compass;
never his partner or his lover or his friend
she is slave to his needs—
i'll pass.
got a sexual appetite of my own,
and i am done spinning webs for anyone but me.
-linda m. crate

bible lesson for misogynists

women who are unmarried
are made to feel as if they are
inferior, somehow,
as if their only worth is found
in a man;
but i am a goddess
full of magic and divinity—
not looking for a ruler or a god
i am a wild thing who must be
appreciated
or i'll just fly away
like any other bird,
i am strong and fiercely independent;
don't need the government
telling me how to live my life—
you can shove these abortion bills
where the sun don't shine
because that's where you'll burn if you
don't mend your ways,
women are not your property;
neither are they your broodmares or incubators—
if you want spiritual guidance
Jesus would tell you to pluck out your eyes.
-linda m. crate

it's not up to you

i have been told by others
"we want more than your rage",
but sometimes that's all i have
when i see the current state of the world;
all those years fighting for women's rights
yet they want to take them away from us—
i don't know about you,
but i don't want to relive times where women were
nothing more than a man's property;
i am over these pompous ignoramuses
that believe they know better than a woman
what to do with her life—
our lives and our dignity mean something
i won't be demeaned by the patriarchy
her choice and her life,
and it's no one's business but her own;
should she answer to anyone
it should not be the government but to herself
and whatever messiah she calls her own
should she—
it is not up to you what people believe,
what religion people practice,
nor anyone's sexuality,
and it certainly is not up to you whether or not a woman
brings a child into this world.
-linda m. crate

let us love them

if a person must make their own choices,
live their own lives,
and dream their own dreams;
then a woman ought to have a right to say
what happens in her life
regardless if you agree with her decision
it is hers and hers alone to make—
will always fight for a person to have that choice
because we were all given free will,
and i refuse to live in a culture where a woman is
enslaved to the needs of the patriarchy;
where she is not able to be who she needs or wants
to be—
we have no right to tell anyone who they are
or who they should be
because only they could know that,
and we have no right to tell someone what to do;
because none of us own another
all we can do is love
for it is the greatest magic we have in this world full
of darkness and chaos sometimes—
let us love one another so hard
that we can let people make their own choices
without judging them because if you're judging someone
it is hard to love them.
-linda m. crate

they don't care about living people

these abortion bans
are just like rape
only about control

they don't care
what a woman has faced
or endured

that she might die
carrying a child to full term
or she may need birth control

to do more than regulate
whether or not to have a baby
they don't care about women

only about the unborn
which they will discard like trash
once they are born

because they are pro-birth
not pro-life,
and they don't care about living people;

just those who might
have a heartbeat
someday.
-linda m. crate

a woman owes no one

they do nothing
about rapists,
they do nothing about
actual threats;
but let's arrest people
and interrogate those who have had
miscarriages—
because the real felons are those
who already suffering,
didn't you know?
it's a messed up system,
and world when a woman is
considered a murderer
for not choosing to have a child for
whatever reason;
and yet a real murderer sometimes
is never caught—
what is wrong with this universe,
and the people who think they have any
right to dictate how people
live their lives if they cannot protect us
from the real monsters,
the real threats,
and the things that could truly kill us?
so please forgive me
but i won't sit idly by and let this evil happen—
i will fight tooth and nail for free will,
and the ability to make one's own choices;
because a woman like the world
owes no one.
-linda m. crate

who is the serpent?

there is a gorgon
who once knew beauty
they say she was a monster,
i say she was betrayed; in the
hour of her need the gods
looked unkindly upon her
punished her for a man's crime.

not much has changed
thousands of years later —
women are still blamed for the sins
of men as if by being by virtue
what and whom we are we enticed
the darkness indwelling from
their hearts to pour out
into the wellspring of life,
and it's disgusting how readily
some swallow this deluge.

were they not born of women? are
there no mothers, sisters, cousins,
nieces, granddaughters, daughters,
lovers, or wives in their lives?

it's evidenced in the bible as this:
a man's nature is to be evil,
but a woman who's lost her spark of
goodness is ten times worse than
that man for her nature is to nurture and love —

then why is it men want to paint her into
a gorgon and make her into witches?
have they not enough idols to burn?

standing on the precipice in time i feel as if
we're going backward instead of forward,
and women's rights is a joke that isn't catching on —
don't stand too close you might catch my
social disease clinging to the tag of the gender
God presented me with at birth.
-linda m. crate

those without substance

who are they to judge us?
our lives and our choices are our own,
and yet they wouldn't give us full
control over our own bodies;
they don't care about women or even
babies
this is all about control—
i am sick of people making this battle into
something it is not,
it is so much more than pro-life or pro-choice;
women's lives are at stake and at risk
yet they would act as if this was what
God wanted—
what right do they have to speak for Him?
God is love,
and they do not know it;
they spew hate and they spew rules
modern day pharisees
throwing stones to break lives and limbs
of those who they see as evil—
they don't understand their houses are made
of glass,
and their lives are easily shattered;
because they have as much substance as
the onion,
but perhaps that's an insult
satire doesn't deserve.
-linda m. crate

you no longer care

your good intentions
mean nothing
the way to hell is stitched
full of them,
you can be well meaning
and still be wrong;
but i cannot imagine how well being
a person can be
if they support abortion
bans—
this is more than
just babies
it's about control,
and the lives that will be lost
should this control be taken;
if you are for life
then you shouldn't be for war—
if you are for life
then you should adopt
one of the many children
sitting in foster care or adoption agencies
in your own country instead of going
abroad;
there are people suffering here
but you don't care about life
just the promise of one;
because once a person is born
you no longer care.
-linda m. crate

we deserve more

you pursue your rules, i pursue justice; you want to paint the world in black and white but i recognize all the shades of gray—i know you think what you're supporting is harmless, it isn't; i have friends who use birth control to regulate their periods, i had a miscarriage and i can only imagination how emotionally unstable i would've been had i had to face an interrogation about what happened; i am sick of women being vilified for living—we each have to live our lives with dignity in whatever matter we deem fit, you may not agree with a woman's choice but she should be able to choose whether or not she will have a child; it's not up to you or the government—your religion shouldn't oppress someone, if it does then maybe you're not practicing properly; God is love and if he is love then He won't judge these people even if they don't always measure up to the standard of your perfection—put down your pitchforks and your rage, can you not see? women are people, too. we deserve dignity, we deserve to be celebrated for our magic and our divinity; we deserve to be loved—we are not property or broodmares, and we deserve more than this world gives us.

-linda m. crate

this isn't black and white

i know you value life
so do i
this is why i cannot support these bans

because it's not about
children as they'd say,
but rather control;

they don't want women to be
seen as people or anything less
than property—

because i value life
i cannot support something
that would end up

killing mothers, sisters, aunts,
daughters, friends, and family;
i cannot support something

that would tear hearts open
because this isn't as black and white
as you want it to be.
-linda m. crate

hypothetical lives

i have seen your silence,
and i raise my rage;
how can you silently condone
this evil?
you know this is wrong,
something in your heart must
whisper to you in the dark;
do you avert your eyes
from seeing truth
in the hopes that embracing
a lie will save you?
these bans will hurt, kill,
and ruin people;
the only lives you care about
are hypothetical—
because the ones pleading,
screaming, shrieking
before you; you ignore—
the lives and hearts that are beating
right now
you're ignoring
for the promise of something
that may or may never be.
-linda m. crate

in case you were wondering

you say you are for life, and if that is so; then why are you not for the lives already living not those yet lived? why are you so opposed to someone making a choice that is none of your business? these bans aren't going to help anyone, and they are only about control; so please forgive me but i am angry—i was told once that "we want more than your rage" but sometimes that is all i can feel for a society so corrupt and callous to the needs of others, you'll say you're for life and yet push for war; you'll say you're for life and let people die on the streets starving—please forgive me if i don't believe you, please forgive me i am incensed, i am burning more brightly than i ever have; i am a forest fire out of control and i am about to burn anyone who thinks a woman owes the world anything simply for existing—we have hopes, dreams, and ambitions of our own; oh yes, and we also have a heartbeat! in case you were wondering.

-linda m. crate

you are the modern day pharisees

i saw someone
share a picture
of a baby in the womb
with the caption
alabama
nothing more,
and it was a man that shared it;
my level of rage was out of this world—
how are you going to condone
a bill that could cause more death
than the lives it would "save"?
i read a story once where a woman was guilted
by the church to have a child the doctor
would say kill her,
and she did only to die afterwards;
the family member was incensed when these
people said it was "God's will"—
judgmental and cruel
you are the modern day pharisees
favoring rules and laws
above people,
but don't fret i am sure your good intentions
will mean something to all those who have died.
-linda m. crate

your life matters to me

i will fight tooth and nail
for a person's right
to choose
because i know
this choice can't be easy,
many things must be considered;
it's not as if people
are selfish and cruel monsters
that do this because they are sick in the head—
whatever your reasoning
i will never judge nor condemn,
and nor should anyone else;
but unfortunately society isn't always kind
they like to paint things in black and white when it isn't
always that simple—
they say they value lives,
but they don't
value yours;
don't worry: i do.
-linda m. crate

they are already here

i'm sorry
your religion isn't enough
to force something
into existence,
and you wouldn't want someone
else ruling over your life
making choices for you when you
have the right to choose;
so why can you not see what you
are doing is wrong?
women are not property
nor are they broodmares or incubators,
and though i could never get an abortion
i won't take that choice from
another woman;
because only they can know what
they've suffered
not you or me—
instead of judgment and hate and the proverbial
life that could be saved,
why cannot you not fight for the lives
that already here?
you don't think they are people fighting
every day for their lives?
save them, save them!
they are already here.
-linda m. crate

it's a pity then that you're wrong

i don't want the government
deciding whether or not i have a child
that is a personal choice,
and why should anyone have the right
to strip us of dignity?
why should anyone get to decide whether
or not a miscarriage was accidental or not?
who are they to judge or know what is in
a person's heart?
they just want felons that cannot vote
so women are yet again stripped
of their voices,
but i refuse to be quiet and slip into a silent night;
i will fight because no one else is
there is so much silence
i feel enraged
my wrath has been provoked by those
who say they value life because you clearly don't
unless it's hypothetical—
the real lives of those already suffering
mean nothing to you,
and those who could die from these ridiculous and unfair
decrees mean nothing to you;
all you care about is yourself and your self-righteousness
that feeling of satisfaction of knowing you're right—
it's a pity then that you're wrong.
-linda m. crate

women are always the villains

they always vilify women
medusa was raped
so they made her the monster,
hera dared to make her own child
so he was ugly
but athena who zeus created on his own
was beautiful;
because how dare a woman exist
in a way that displeases
someone
or do something a man disapproves of?
how dare a woman not give into the wants
or desires of a man?
i am sick of society
always blaming women
for everything that is wrong in this universe,
we are not your moral compasses
nor your angels;
we are not your property or your punching bags
nor are we your broodmares—
we should have the right to make choices
in our own lives and over our own bodies,
and since all woman who are wild are
considered villains
you may as well as add me to the list;
but i am proud to be a villain
if to be a hero
you must enforce your will.
-linda m. crate

you don't value life

i fight for what is right,
and what i feel
is right is to allow people
the free will to make their own choices;
you may not agree with it
but i doubt everyone would agree
with all your private decisions
yet no one villifies you for simply existing—
a woman can make a choice
you don't agree with,
and still be a good person;
no matter what you may be led to believe—
i feel if you were really for life
then you would put more time and energy
in preventing wars,
feeding the homeless,
taking care of the widows,
adopting children not only from abroad
but those suffering in your own country,
and you would care that there are children being torn
from the arms of their loving families;
but since you are quiet on all these things
i think we can safely assume
you don't value life
just control.
-linda m. crate

you do not value women

in a world that sometimes makes people feel small, why must we go out of our way to make people feel smaller? shrieking murderer at someone who got an abortion when there are actual murderers roaming the street and killing people doesn't make you some sort of hero or angel sent from God, it just makes you a person screaming at someone who probably had to make one of the most difficult choices of their lives; you don't know what's happening in a person's life and yet you feel so justified in judging them—you call them the villains but you forget your fingers aren't clean and you aren't free of sin, but instead of pulling the plank from your own eyes you are so busy judging them for the speck in their eyes; in a world where even God gives us free will you would take it away, for what? some sense of superiority? you say you value life, you value control; you only value lives whose vision aligns with yours, you do not value women.

-linda m. crate

i refuse to be caged

a woman doesn't owe anything
just because she exists
in case you didn't get the memo
a woman owes you nothing
just because you find her attractive
in case you didn't know
because there seem to be a lot of
things you don't,
a woman's life is her own;
she should be able to make her own choices
only she has to face the consequences of her actions—
doesn't need the self-righteous or the government
making the choice for her
or telling her she is a horrible person,
the only terrible people are the ones in power who think they
have any right to tell others how to live their lives;
you don't want religious dogma forced on you
and yet you would force someone else's hand into
oppression?
no.
you don't seem to understand this goes beyond
pro-life and pro-choice,
they want to control women;
and i refuse to be caged.
-linda m. crate

will never be their songbird

all my life
they've tried to cage me,
and make me small;
tell me that i need a man to truly
live my life as i ought,
but i am not ready to recoil a small
rabbit and surrender my power;
simply so a man can keep
his ego—
i am not inferior
to men
just because they fear
my power
i am magic, i am love, i am light;
and i will shatter all their
hollow nightmares and bones of monsters
beneath my rage for my
kindness is no
weakness—
i will not stand down because they want
me to stand upon pedestals,
be tamed,
have their children;
be comfortable behind gilded cages that break
my soul and dreams into oblivion's dust—
i am wild
burning like fire,
and i will never be tamed;
their assured cages and chains will fail them

when they try to catch me like a butterfly in their net
it will snare across their fingers to break them
for i am a hurricane i will break down all their walls
shatter their glass ceilings
i am the wind i will take all their words and cut them
down to pieces with their hostility
i am the earth
will quake beneath their feet and destroy everything
they once loved for daring to stomp on the dreams and rights
of women
i am steel
my ambition will pierce them until the crows
fall from the heavens to devour their bones.
-linda m. crate

we will not be destroyed

it is exhausting
to always
fight,
but i cannot rescind
my fury from
this battle;
for there is too much at risk—
too many people think
it's simply a difference of opinion
between pro-birth and pro-life,
don't know how to open their eyes
to show them this is about
control;
they want to tell us what to do
in our lives in this way
then they will continue to oppress us
until we have no rights—
i will not let them take an inch
let alone a mile,
i will not be oppressed by people
who do not understand
that women are more than mothers;
we are so strong, so powerful, so capable
and we will not be destroyed
by the patriarchy.
-linda m. crate

you will not control me
i am not here
for your consumption
or entertainment

i am here
to live my life,
create a new world;

a world where
women are seen as equals
not inferiors—

i am here
to be more than a broodmare,
wife, or mother;

i am here to accomplish
all my dreams
i refuse to surrender myself

for the sake of anyone
you will not control me
simply because i exist.
-linda m. crate

we were all given free will

i won't feel guilty for fighting for those who make a choice you disagree with, i won't feel guilty for demanding women be treated as people and not property; you care more about a hypothetical person than the woman or the struggle she's suffered—i am sure it wasn't easy for her to make this decision, it's probably the only choice she feels she have; and i won't let you take that from her—oppressing someone for the greater good isn't good, there is no greater good; can you not see when one suffers we all do? these abortion bans have to do with more than just a person's stance on pro-life and pro-birth, and to know so many will be silent in the face of this evil disgusts me; you are not a good person if you oppress others simply because you feel they are wrong and you are right—we were all given free will, and i will not surrender mine nor hers or anyone else's simply so you can be a self-righteous pharisee keen on enforcing all your rules.

-linda m. crate

i refuse to be oppressed

a woman is a woman
even if she chooses
to be a mother
even if she doesn't
a woman is a woman
even if she chooses to marry
or she doesn't,
she is no one's property;
nor is she a broodmare
or incubator—
her choice and her dignity
should be her own to make,
there shouldn't be inquiries to face
should she have a miscarriage;
no one is to blame
she is not at fault—
we were not meant to live
our lives in fear or bondage,
i refuse to be oppressed;
will fight tooth and nail
so we can all keep our rights.
-linda m. crate

they already have heartbeats

you think you'll stop abortions?
only safe ones.
these bans aren't to save babies,
but to enslave women
to the needs of the patriarchy;
and who are they to decide
what choices we make?
our lives and our dignity belong
to us
not them,
and i refuse to be oppressed;
i refuse to accept that this is the
only way or the right way—
you don't see the blood that
will be on your hands
if you do this,
or maybe you simply don't care;
but you should—
these women you're trying to force
into submission
already have heartbeats,
they have dreams and purpose;
and they can make choices for themselves
even if you disagree with their choice
they ought to have the right to decide their
own fate.
-linda m. crate

i will fight for justice

i will never see eye-to-eye with people who claim to be pro-life when they are only pro-birth, i will always be pro-choice because i believe it is none of our business what someone does in their own life; and i will forever choose to allow people to live their own lives rather than to dictate their every movement because if God gave us all free will then who is any man to attempt to take this away from us? i refuse to accept your truth as *the* truth because the two are very different things, and if you could only see how your blinders are refusing to let you see the whole picture maybe you would realize how very wrong these bills are; you don't have to agree or want an abortion—but you shouldn't stop people from living their lives how they see ought, it is not up to you if they choose your religion or your gods, it is not up to you if they should see life the way you do; if you unblocked the lenses of your eyes perhaps you would see things more clearly—there's not need to be hostile, but if you want a war; i will fight for justice not rules.

-linda m. crate

open up your eyes

if no one can walk their own path
then we have no right to call ourselves
humane,
because how can we choose life
at the risk of the death of others?
single-minded point of view
you can't seem to scrape together
this is more than an issue of morality,
it is an issue of people trying
to control other people;
seeing women as something less
than a person
incapable of making a decision in her own life—
open up your eyes
see the truth
even if it is a hard pill to swallow,
another person's choice is none of your business;
we cannot control other people
each of us was given free will
have to make our own fate
cannot let anyone anchor us down to a life
that isn't ours to live.
-linda m. crate

so leave her alone

i will speak loudly
because all my life i felt
compelled to silence,
holding my tongue
lest i offend;
but i am a daughter of the moon
i was born to make waves
refuse to silence myself
any longer—
you want to paint the world
in black and white
refusing to accept there are
shades of gray,
you want to make it all about
the choice on the surface
of the problem
rather than the entirety of
the truth;
a woman should have control
over her own life
she shouldn't feel trapped in her own body—
a woman is no one's property,
she is not a broodmare or incubator,
and she will always be powerful and magical
regardless whether or not
she makes the choice you approve of;
because she is here to have her own life and dignity
you don't want stripped of yours
so leave her alone.
-linda m. crate

you aren't better than anyone else

you want to see a woman as a virgin, whore, or crone; you don't want to consider all the shades between—you want to open certain pages of the bible whilst ignoring others, you want to point out all the sins of others yet be forgiven for your own; you want to oppress and destroy women all in the name of "life"—i am done listening to the pointless, idle arguments of people who refuse to see the whole of the picture; you can love Jesus and still be pro-choice—if you think a person should have no right to live their own life then tell me why God gave you free will, and if you want that free will then stop trying to take it away from others; it's that simple—you may not agree with a person's decision but it is their life to live not yours—if you don't want an abortion then don't have one, but don't take away that option for those who feel that's their only choice; if you truly want to be a good person you should recognize this worlds need more love and less judgment—you aren't better than anyone else.

-linda m. crate

you can't force the "right" choice

a woman
is not less than a man
so i refuse to
accept
these bans
who would reduce a
living, breathing being
to an incubator
against her will;
we have no right to dictate
how others live their
lives—
this is a choice she has to
make for herself
stripping dignity from a person
based on your religious beliefs
doesn't make you a moral person
just an oppressive one
forcing someone to make the "right"
decision even for the right reasons is still wrong—
a person must be free to live their own lives,
women don't owe anyone simply for existing;
and so you cannot expect your demands are going
to go unchecked or without question.
-linda m. crate

i will never accept that

who are you to decide?
you have no right
to dictate the choice
someone makes in their own lives,
keep your babies
if you are against abortion;
but don't expect everyone to make
the same choice
and don't try to force anyone's hand—
you are not gods but men,
and what right do you have to demand
someone live by the laws
of your religion
when you wouldn't want to live
by the rules of anyone else's?
i will fight always
for the right of a woman to choose,
becaue it's not up to you or i
how someone lives their life;
and you should know that by now
these bans are only about controlling people
i will never accept that—
no one should be caged by the desires
or needs of another,
we all need to be free to decide
our own lives.
-linda m. crate

we are so much more than this
you want the forgiveness
that you would withhold
from these women should they
decide for themselves they don't
want to give birth,
you are the very evil you claim
that you don't want on this
earth;
i do not understand how you are
so blind as you cannot see
all the people who would die from
your decision—
don't want to be controlled,
but you do want control over the womb
of a woman you don't even know?
that's messed up,
and we all know it;
just admit it you're not pro-life
you're anti-choice and pro-birth and you
have never cared for women—
you only see them as
carries for children,
but we are so much more than this.
-linda m. crate

a woman shouldn't have to abandon herself

from the time i was sixteen up
people in my small town kept pushing
boyfriends and marriage and motherhood
as if these were the only things
i should want in life,
as if i should abandon my dreams;
settle for a life i knew wasn't for me—
which isn't to say
one day i might not be married or have children,
but i would not be satisfied with a simple life
want adventures and escapes into the wild that whispers
to my heart—
a woman shouldn't have to abandon herself to make
society happy,
a woman shouldn't be expected to forgo
who she is
strictly to fit some arbitrary requirement for society—
we are who we are,
some of us are willing to be oppressed;
but some of us, like me, demand to have choices—
i won't surrender my free will nor that of anyone else
simply to please society,
women aren't here to fit your standards and accomplish your
aims;
our lives and our destinies are our own to fulfill.
-linda m. crate

treat others as you would treat yourself

just because you wouldn't do it doesn't mean you have any right to tell someone else not to, everyone has to be free to live their own lives as they see fit; no one is forced to see things from your point of view or through the lens of your religion of choice—if you don't like abortions then don't get one, but you don't get to oppress others and force them to live the way you see as right; what is right for you may not be right for someone else and you have to respect that even if you don't necessarily like it—it is not your choice whether or someone has a child or not, and so i will never stand by these bans; i will always fight for a person's right to choose their own lives—i accept people for who they are, appreciate them even if they make choices i may not agree with, and i love people even if they are different than i am; because we should all live and let live—if you don't want to be oppressed then don't oppress others, treat others as you would treat your-self.

-linda m. crate

stop throwing your stones

stop seeing
them as the faceless horde
of evil villains
simply trying to eradicate
the human race
because it's the woman you
went to high school with that was
raped,
it is the woman you work with
that has to get an abortion so she
can get her chemo treatments,
it is the woman who
goes to your church who will die
if she doesn't get one;
try some empathy
instead of caring about hypothetical
people
care about the ones already here—
life is already hard enough
without having to face the judgment
of others,
and who has no sin?
i see a lot of people casting
stones,
but the bones of those you break;
they are the ones earning favor with heaven
because blowing out someone else's candle
doesn't light yours.
-linda m. crate

they're not devils

we won't throw in the white flag
there is no surrendering
we won't become
ghosts,
but we will haunt your steps;
women are not your property
nor your broodmares
or incubators—
a woman must be able to decide
for herself what her life
will be,
and regardless of your stance
you should be appalled at how
extreme and vile these
bans are;
of how many people could possibly die
from such a thing—
but you don't care do you?
you've already deemed them villains,
painted them in a shade of black;
made them devils
with sharp teeth
instead of a woman put in a position
only she could know the struggle of.
-linda m. crate

a time for war

you want to keep your freedoms, then why take them away from us? women are not here to be entertainment or broodmares, we are not here to simply be brides and mothers; we are divine and magical beings—you will disrespect us no longer, we are done being the targets of your rage simply because you fear or abhor our power; the silence is deafening when it comes to the support of women—makes me wonder how you treat your own wives, daughters, mothers, aunts, sisters, and female friends; i cannot imagine well if you would see them surrender their rights and their dignity—can you not see that they want all women to be felons so none of us can vote? or perhaps you support that. regardless, i am repulsed by the fact that no one seems to care that people are or will be suffering because of these bans; i will be a voice for the voiceless—i refuse to relent, i refuse to calm down, i refuse to surrender my rage, there is a time for peace; but right now is a time for war.

-linda m. crate

you're blinded by your feelings

no one should face shame
for making a decision in her own life
even if you disagree with it
there should be no judgment,
your religion gives you no excuse to
be an ass to others;
nor will we be willing to accept this
as an excuse—
men were never meant to be
above us
we were created to be equals,
might does not make right;
and i will not support these bans
because this personal choice has no right being
decided by the government—
a woman's life and her dignity are
her own,
she must choose her own path;
i won't let you fools take that away from her
because you're so blinded by your
feelings
that you cannot see that you are wrong.
-linda m. crate

you're practicing wrong

"everyone just wants to see you settle down"
oh, but i grow wilder with age;
i just have this sensibility that everyone should
be given the freedom to make their own
decisions in their own life—
i will fight tooth and nail to make it thus
because who has any right to stop us from
living our lives as we deem we ought?
i was always taught to keep the peace,
but sometimes we need to make waves;
i won't stand idly by look evil in the eyes
doing nothing about it
i will fight—
should they be given an inch
they will take a mile,
and i am not going to let that happen;
i am not going to surrender myself as a sacrificial lamb
for the hordes in the patriarchy
who see nothing wrong with
oppressing people—
if your religion requires you to be cruel or to hate
you're practicing wrong.
-linda m. crate

these women have faces

it is none of your business
what another person
does in their lives,
and guilting them into making a choice
that will be permanent in their lives
is wrong;
forcing their hands to give birth
to a child they have no interest in
also wrong—
because once a child is born
you no longer care
pro-birth not pro-life
because if you were there would be
no famines, there would be no war,
and no one would even care who went missing
there wouldn't more attention on the pretty
white girl than the pretty indigenous girl;
if you were pro-life there would be no starving
homeless people buried in the snow—
if you care about women
you would see
this for what it really is
oppression
presented as life saving
when really it is a black hand of death whose scythe
is at the throat of these women
you imagine don't have faces
but she's your sister, your daughter,
your family, your friend;
and she is begging you for her life.
-linda m. crate

don't really believe in life, do you?

if you truly believed in life
you would plant more
trees,
you would take care of the
environment and the only earth
we have as home;
you would realize that we already
have a population crisis—
if you truly believed in life
there would be no war,
and you wouldn't let homeless
people go without homes or food;
you wouldn't let people starve
from lack of love or affection
you would care—
instead you would shackle a woman
to the needs of the patriarchy,
strip her of all her rights,
force her
to beget every child no matter the
cost to her life or how it may shatter
her family into pieces;
i wish you could see what you were doing
maybe then you would reconsider.
-linda m. crate

i cannot forgive nightmares or hell

women are not your property,
and they're not your broodmares;
you are not entitled to our
lives or our bodies!
we should be the only ones
deciding
what our lives will be,
i won't support the goverment
putting their hands on another facet
of our lives;
they say they will protect us
if we kneel
well, i have a problem with that
they are not my gods and they are not
my friends and they are against me
not for me—
i will never kneel for anyone
let alone men who think that women
should have a child no matter
the cost to their bodies or sanity,
i won't forgive men
who would take that choice away from us;
neither will i the women who silently stand by
or quietly agree with evil
because i cannot forgive nightmares or hell.
-linda m. crate

we were never inferiors

you want protection from
the government
in the form of your guns,
but you would allow that same
government
to strip a woman of her rights
simply in the name of life?
have i got that right?
i despise hypocrisy—
when you choose life do you
also get to choose which lives
matter more?
because you will always choose
the hypothetical child no matter what,
why is it that the unborn
deserve more rights than the living
who already have heartbeats?
you want protection from the government,
i want protection from mankind;
because none of them seem to have any
good intentions
when it comes to women—
no woman owes you a thing for existing,
we are not broodmares or conquests;
you have no right to treat us so poorly
we were never inferiors.
-linda m. crate

battle ready wild birds

why should you thirst
to rule over women with an iron fist?
do you not see all the suffering
in the world today?
can you really blame someone
for not wanting to bring a child into
the chaos of our nightmarish song?
we are not your slaves,
broodmares,
incubators,
moral compasses,
or angels;
we are living and breathing entities
full of dreams and ambitions
of our own—
we're not here for your entertainment,
and we're not your property;
i don't know why you think we will all
relinquish our rights without thought
because not all of us
are lambs ready to be led to slaughter
some of us are battle ready wild birds ready
to take the eyes of those swinging the axes
freeing the sheep to live another day.
-linda m. crate

whether you like it or not

you need to calm down
stop taking it personally
people are allowed to make
their own choices,
and live their own lives;
the fact of the matter is
unless it touches you personally
you should probably keep your nose
out of other people's business—
if your religion requires
you hate or oppress someone
maybe you need a new one
(or to practice properly)
so take a few seats
because women are done being
your punching bags and broodmares,
and you may not agree with
the choice someone makes;
its okay
don't think everyone agrees with yours—
live and let live
because people are going to decide
what is right for their lives whether you like it or not.
-linda m. crate

we can all be monsters

chill out!
no one's forcing you to have
an abortion
if you don't want one,
but should someone need to have
one
they should have that choice;
we were all born with free will
our decisions for our own lives are our own—
you don't own women,
and you don't get to decide
what we do in our own lives;
i refuse to accept the cage of these bans
will fight fang and claw
because we can all be monsters
i am done playing nice
with people who want to oppress or kill
me or my fellow women
because we all deserve the chance
to live our best lives,
and you never know what someone is going through
less judgment and more love please
try to understand where someone is coming from
people who want abortions aren't
evil villains or monsters without faces
they're people like you and me
(if some of you can even call yourselves people).
-linda m. crate

sometimes life gives us no choice

i'm going to fight
on the side of justice

you with all your rules,
i wonder do you ever
get tired?

i am exhausted of fighting evil,
but i will never stop fighting for good;
there are too many lives on the line
going to use my heart as a weapon of war
against every wicked thing i see—

you may think nothing about these
abortion bans,
but that's what they want;

they don't want you to see the risk
until they've gutted us of all our
rights
i cannot let that happen
neither should you—

do you understand how much
blood will be on your hands should you choose
to allow them to oppress women,
do you understand that we're not angry
for the sake of being enraged?

one would think we'd want to spend our
energy being anything other than outraged about politics,
but sometimes life gives us no choice.
-linda m. crate

you feel the need to oppress others

this little light of mine,
i'm going to let it shine;
will illuminate the eyes
of any willing to
listen—
you say you are pro-life,
and i must ask
if you are in opposition
of war?
do you feed and clothe and try to
house the homeless?
do you care about those suffering?
otherwise you're just pro-birth,
and anti-choice,
pro-suffering and anti-women;
because these abortion bans cover more
than just abortion—
and the morning after pill
helps regulate the hormones of some
of my friends and their cycles,
but you would take this away from them
simply because you feel the need to oppress others
with your religion?
i may be going out on a limb here,
but i don't think that's what Jesus would do.
-linda m. crate

we won't let this go

we won't sink
like treasure ships of old,
we will rise
like air above all our oppressors;
and i know you think
you're doing the right
thing
yet that doesn't mean that you are—
this abortion ban
was even opposed by a
televangelist,
and if that doesn't tell you how bad
it is
then i don't know what will;
it is not about protecting children as they
would have you believe—
it is about controlling women,
and that isn't fair;
because no one tries to control men
or tell them not to have sex or close their legs
every unwanted pregnancy is caused
by a man—
so maybe stop trying to oppress and control people
we weren't born to fit into your boxes or cages,
and we have no intention of letting this go.
-linda m. crate

it isn't about babies

you're passionate for those unborn,
but what about those already here?
do you fight for them, too?
if you value women,
then why are you so keen on
drowning their voices out unless they
agree with you?
you could never know their pain
or their necessity in making such a decision,
but you would deny them it for the sake
of life;
but if you valued lives then would there
really be so much suffering and strife in this world?
you cannot tell me you care about life,
and then strike food from the hands of the homeless;
you cannot tell me you care about life,
and then let a woman die for lack of chemotherapy
because of the orphan she can give this world—
it isn't about babies, it's about control;
plain and simple
i am not willing to relinquish the rights of myself
or my sisters—
i refuse to accept that we cannot do better than this.
-linda m. crate

more than our circumstances

we want it all:
success, freedom, respect,
dignity, intelligence,
common sense and common decency;
you don't have to see it from my
perspective completely
just understand this is a lot deeper
an issue than it appears
when you skim the surface—
i know you want those who get
abortions to be faceless villains who
you can condemn to hell,
but let's face it;
it's the girl you saw with tears staining
her eyes at the grocery store
or the woman who averted her eyes
at the doctor's office because she felt
you'd judge her if you knew,
it's the girl who you went to high school with
and thought she was so smart,
she is the friend who always makes you laugh—
we want to be more than our circumstances,
and sometimes that means making
difficult decisions.
-linda m. crate

you choose to be blind

reproductive rights should be just that: rights, everyone was given the free-will to choose their path; why should that be taken away from us simply because people want a war? because if you didn't want someone to hate then you wouldn't be making these bans, if you didn't want an uprising then you wouldn't think you could control someone this way; but you remain silent when they try to take our reproductive rights away—well, if it is wrong for them to take your guns please explain to me how it's wrong for us to have the choice over what happens in our own lives? are our bodies not our own? do we not have the right to reject motherhood? why should it be forced upon someone who doesn't want it? are there not enough unwanted children in this world? abused, hurt, ridiculed, rejected, wounded, angry, confused people who suffer simply because they exist; and you would wish that upon another? what kind of evil are you? you have eyes to see yet you choose to be blind.

-linda m. crate

i have so much rage, as is

don't take the pill
never mind it does more
than just prevent pregnancies,
you have no agency
to your bodies or your bodily functions;
let your hormones go out of control
prove to the world how crazy women
truly are—
i am sick of living in this universe
where women have no rights,
and are only seen as property and objects
of immediate sexual gratification;
some are blissfully unaware of this war raging
beneath the surface
i cannot keep quiet
remain silent
about this subject burning on my mind—
i have so much rage, as it is,
and this is just another thing to make
me feel the warmth of anger
burn like a forest fire inside me;
i refuse to stand in line and wait for my turn
to have my rights taken away—
i will spit in the face of anyone who seeks
to control me,
i am not someone you can tame;
and i refuse your cages and your rules
i will live my life and fulfill my destiny
without anyone telling me how i should live my life—

i won't relent, i won't give up, and i will not give in;
maybe you don't know this about me
but i am underestimated in my strength
no one really knows how deep the anger lies.
-linda m. crate

i have little faith in them

i don't understand
why you need more control?
people are denied medications
to cure their depression,
so i suppose it makes sense you
would refuse
to believe women who want abortions as anything
less than evil;
you don't understand
that it is more than what they want you to see
on the surface or perhaps you've considered and
you still think it's wrong—
it is okay,
but how can you tell the woman who needs
chemotherapy she is wrong
for wanting to live?
or the mother who already has more children
than she can afford that she must take the obligation
of another?
how can you tell us that we don't deserve our freedom?
it is called reproductive rights for a reason,
and i will always fight for myself and my sisters;
you may think this is an unholy war—
if you're going to judge people,
have you seen the sins of your clergy?
i have little faith in them.
-linda m. crate

they are devils not gods

hell is empty
all the devils are dancing here
telling us
we need more control and restraint
they think their pretty little
rules make them look like prophets
because they know
the bible, too;
and they like to recite a verse every now and again
so you'll nod your head and agree they're good
people—
let me tell you this
good people
don't oppress others,
good people
consider others may make choices they disagree with
and they meet these people with love not anger;
so until you release your pitchforks
i won't release my rage
seems a fair trade
when you want to tie me in restraints—
i refuse to be anyone's captive,
just let us have our reproductive rights;
you do not need to control nor rule us—
can you not see they are devils
not gods?
-linda m. crate

our lives are our own

you'll say there are two sides
of the story yet refuse to listen to
those who are in favor
of what you consider evil,
but true evils exist in this world
you do not even try to fight;
and i do not comprehend—
the key to understanding
is unlocking close-mindness
to fathoming your point of view
may not be the right one,
your good intentions and your faith
aren't enough excuse
to oppress others
who refuse to see your point of view;
can you blame them?
you insist they surrender their bodies and their rights
simply so they can suffer and die
pregnancy is complicated even in the best circumstances
things can go wrong,
and why should anyone have to surrender anything?
we were all born with free will,
and we refuse to surrender it;
let us choose our fate and live our lives as we must
some of you will say we make the right choice and others
the wrong choice
yet we will all make the right decision for us—
our lives are our own.
-linda m. crate